Woven Celtic Knots

Nacho Grandma's Quilts

Raymond K. Houston

Blue Dragon Publishing

Woven Celtic Knots

by Raymond K. Houston

All rights reserved.

Published by Blue Dragon Publishing, LLC

Lightfoot, VA

www.blue-dragon-publishing.com

Copyright 2018 Raymond K. Houston

ISBN 978-1-939696-38-0 (paperback)

ISBN 978-1-939696-39-7 (eBook)

Photographs by Scott Lokitz

CRA031000 Crafts & Hobbies / Quilts & Quilting

CRA061000 Crafts & Hobbies / Fiber Arts & Textiles

For your convenience, we post an up-to-date listing of corrections on our website (www.Blue-Dragon-Publishing.com). If a correction is not already noted, please email us at info@blue-dragon-publishing.com.

Printed in the U.S.A.

Table of Contents

To all the Joans in my life.

Introduction

I am a textile artist, and Celtic knots fascinate me. I love the way their paths twist and turn in endless, interwoven loops.

I have developed a neat and simple method for making Celtic knots. I cut the paths of the knot as a loop or chain of loops, then weave them together.

The result is an elegant Woven Celtic Knot.

Woven Celtic Knot Band, Style A, Filler One

This book shows how to weave simple Celtic knot bands, boxes, and crosses using my method. Seventeen interchangeable knot templates are included so you can create original Celtic knots, or you can use Celtic knots from other sources such as coloring books.

This is a very versatile method and works with either paper or fabric. It works with a variety of applique techniques, such as raw edge fusible, freezer paper, or needle-turned applique.

Use the knots to embellish table linens, quilts, or clothing.

Library of Knots

When I first started working with Celtic knots, I tried drawing them. That was too labor-intensive for my purposes, and the results were inconsistent. I needed an easy way to draw uniform Celtic knots.

I bought a computer font that lets me draw consistent knots with just a few keystrokes. I used the font to create this set of templates.

There are six styles of knots, lettered A through F. Each style is represented by Knot Corners and Knot Ends.

Knot Corners

Knot Corners are open along two adjacent sides.

Style A	Style B	Style C	Style D	Style E	Style F

Four Knot Corners form a Celtic knot box. All six styles combine to generate 1,296 different combinations of boxes (which I won't show for obvious reasons).

Style A	Style B	Style C

Style D	Style E (with Style C)	Style F

Knot Ends

Knot Ends are open along one side. Style A and Style E exhibit two opposing paths. Style B and Style D exhibit one path enclosing another path. Style C and Style F exhibit one path linked through another path. All six styles combine to generate 21 unique knots.

	Style A	Style B	Style C	Style D	Style E	Style F
Style A						
Style B						
Style C						
Style D						
Style E						
Style F						

Knot Fillers

There are five Knot Fillers, numbered One through Five. Knot Fillers are open along two opposite sides, except for Filler Five which is open along all four sides. They provide length to the knots. They also affect the shape of the paths. The paths may look one way with an odd number of fillers between the Knot Ends and Knot Corners; they may look another way with an even number of fillers.

Filler One	Filler Two	Filler Three	Filler Four	Filler Five

The following charts show how the number of Knot Fillers between Knot Ends and Knot Corners affects the shape of the paths.

Filler One

Style A	Style B	Style C	Style D	Style E	Style F

Filler One (continued)

Style A	Style B	Style C

Style D	Style E (with Style C)	Style F

Style A	Style B	Style C	Style D	Style E	Style F

Filler Two (continued)

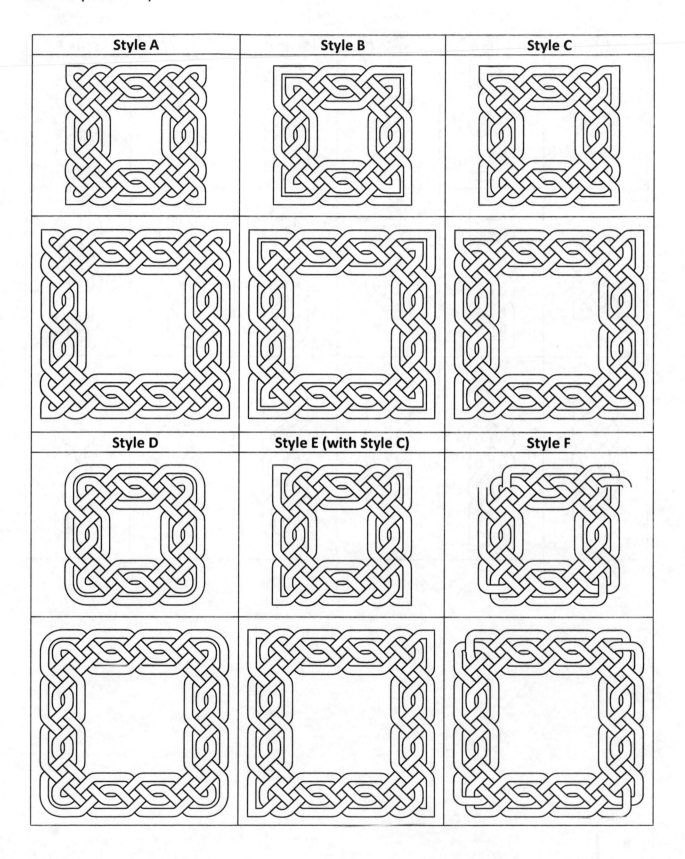

Filler Three

Style A	Style B	Style C	Style D	Style E	Style F

Filler Three (continued)

Style A	Style B	Style C

Style D	Style E (with Style C)	Style F

Filler Four

Filler Four introduces a break in the path. Use two or more fillers to separate unbroken paths.

Style A	Style B	Style C	Style D	Style E	Style F

Filler Four (continued)

Style A	Style B	Style C

Style D	Style E (with Style C)	Style F

Filler Five

Filler Five combined with Knot Ends appears as crosses. You can lengthen the cross arms by adding additional Fillers One through Four.

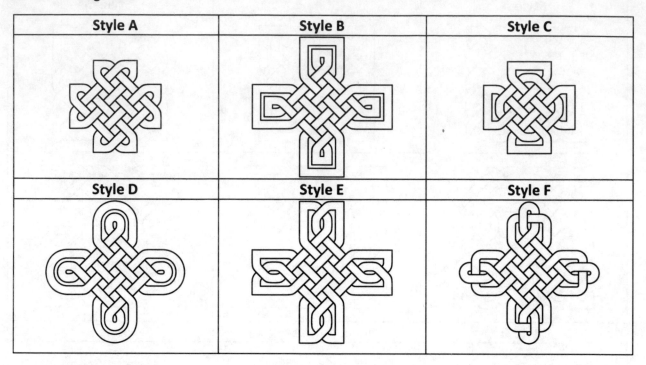

The crosses look like this with the addition of Filler One.

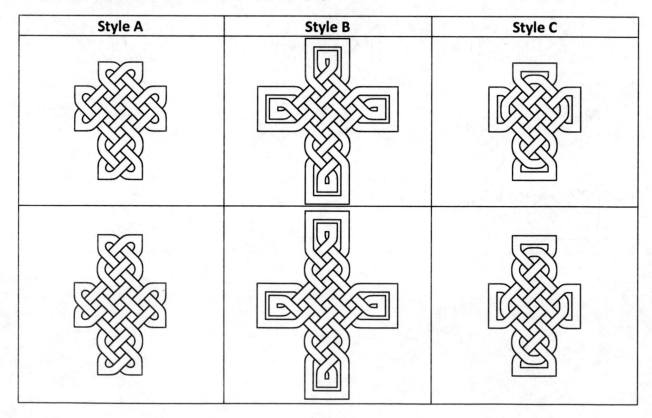

The crosses look like this with the addition of Filler Two.

Style A	Style B	Style C

Style D	Style E	Style F

The crosses look like this with the addition of Filler Three.

Style A	Style B	Style C

Style D	Style E	Style F

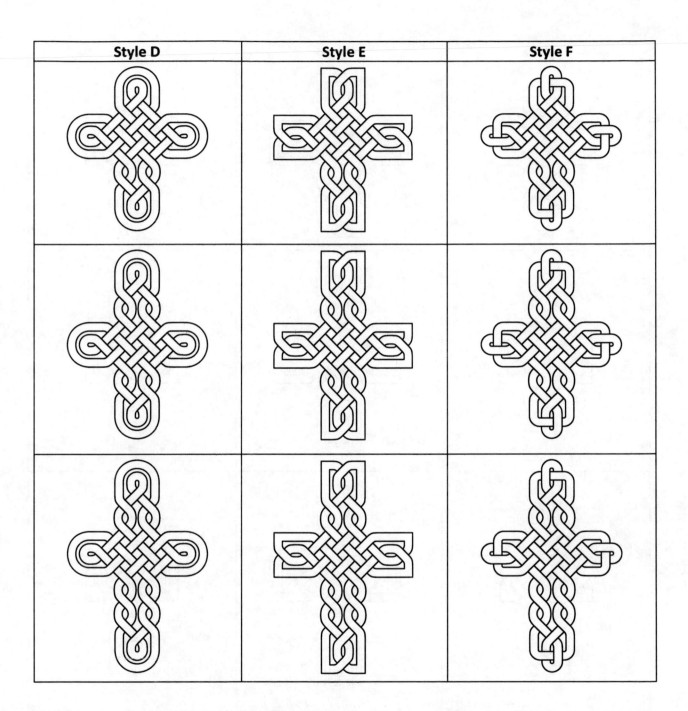

The crosses look like this with the addition of Filler Four.

Style A	Style B	Style C

Style D	Style E	Style F

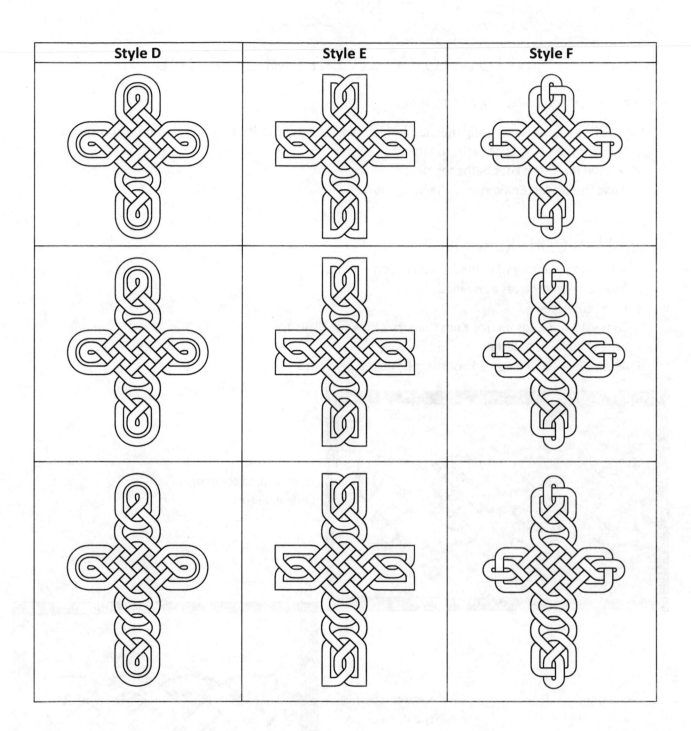

How to Weave a Celtic Knot

There are four steps in weaving a Celtic knot.

I. Assemble a Celtic knot using the included templates or use a Celtic knot from another source
II. Transfer the Celtic knot paths to fabric
III. Weave the Celtic knot paths together
IV. Fuse the woven Celtic knot to its background

Assemble a Celtic Knot

1. Refer to the Library of Knots for inspiration
2. Photocopy templates as needed
3. Trim templates
4. Connect Knot Ends and/or Knot Corners with Knot Fillers to suit
5. Tape templates together
6. Assemble a second Celtic knot using Reversed Templates.

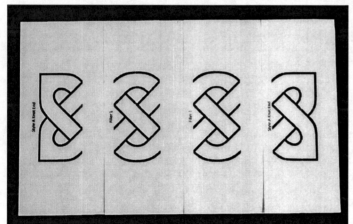

Photocopied templates,
Style A, Filler One

Assembled templates,
Style A, Filler One

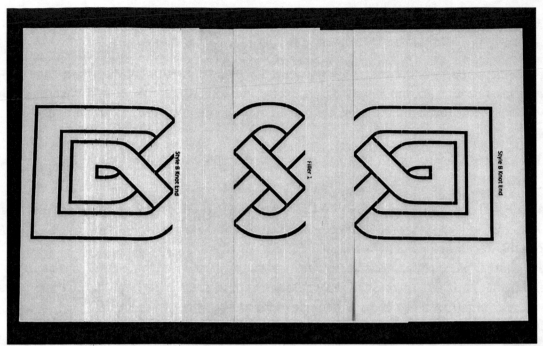

Photocopied templates, Style B, Filler One

Assembled templates, Style B, Filler One

Transfer the Celtic Knot

Assemble Celtic knots as shown above. Use the Reversed Templates knot for tracing.

Identify the separate paths of the knot. They travel from one end of the knot to the other. They often cross over themselves, resulting in what looks like a chain of loops. Some combinations of templates produce a single-path Celtic knot. You cannot use this method on those knots. You need two or more paths to weave them together.

Transfer the paths of the knot to fabric using paper-backed fusible web. Feel free to adopt and adapt to suit yourself.

1. Place paper-backed fusible web on top of reversed template. Trace along both edges of a single path, even across the gap where the path crosses "under" another path (even itself).
2. Move the traced outline out of the way.
3. Place another piece of paper-backed fusible web on top of reversed template. Trace along both edges of the other path, even across the gap where the path crosses "under" another path (even itself).
4. Fuse the two path outlines to the wrong side of fabric.
5. Trim away the outer and inner outlines and remove the paper backing.

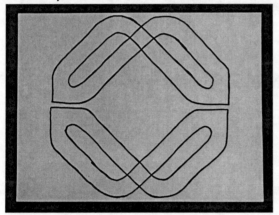

Traced paths, Style A, Filler One

Fused and trimmed paths, Style A, Filler One

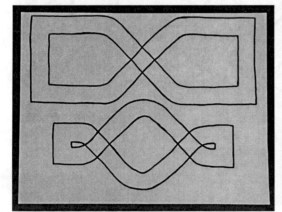

Traced paths, Style B, Filler One

Fused and trimmed paths, Style B, Filler One

Weave a Celtic Knot Band
(All Styles)

Assemble a Celtic knot and transfer the paths to fabric as shown above.

The paths of a Celtic knot band are generally chains of closed loops that have to be cut open before weaving them together. The best place to cut open a path is where it crosses under another path.

Use the assembled templates as a placement guide.

1. Position a fused and trimmed path on the placement guide. Pin it to the placement guide to anchor it in place at an intersection where the path crosses itself.

Fused and trimmed path pinned to placement guide, Style A, Filler One

2. Position and pin the other fused and trimmed path to the placement guide to anchor it in place at an intersection where the path crosses itself.
3. It is best to start at the center of the knot and weave toward the ends. Cut open loops (only once) as needed and weave them, pinning the fabric layers together. Use two pins to hold the two cut edges. Use the placement guide to help determine which path to weave under and over.

Fused and trimmed paths woven and pinned together, Style A, Filler One

4. Run a finger above each path to check the overs and unders. The rule of thumb is if a path goes over the first path it encounters, it goes under the next path it encounters (even itself).
5. When completely woven and pinned together, the knot acts as a single unit. Unpin the fabric layers from the placement guide but keep the fabric layers pinned together.
6. Position the knot on its background.
7. Remove the pins and fuse the knot in place.
8. Stitch around the outlines of the knot.

Fused and trimmed path pinned to placement guide
Style B, Filler One

Fused and trimmed paths woven and pinned together,
Style B, Filler One

Woven Celtic Knot Band, Style B, Filler One

Weave a Celtic Knot Cross

(All Styles)

Assemble a Celtic knot and transfer the paths to fabric as shown previously.

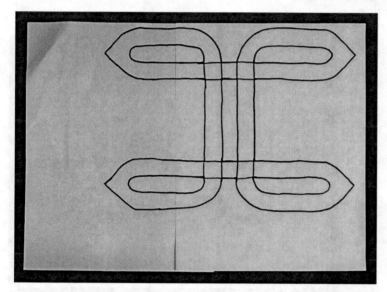

Traced paths, Style A, Fillers One and Five

Fused and trimmed paths, Style A, Fillers One and Five

The paths of a Celtic knot cross are generally chains of closed loops that have to be cut open before weaving them together. The best place to cut open a path is where it crosses under another path.

Use the assembled templates as a placement guide.

It is best to start at the center of the knot and weave outward along the arms.

1. Lay a fused and trimmed path on the placement guide.

Fused and trimmed path positioned on placement guide,
Style A, Fillers One and Five

2. Lay the other fused and trimmed path on top of the first.

Fused and trimmed paths positioned on placement guide, Style A, Fillers One and Five

3. Pin the paths together through all layers of fabric and paper to anchor them at the center, cutting open one path where it crosses under another path before weaving them together. Use two pins to hold the two cut edges.
4. Working outward along the arms of the knot, cut open loops (only once) as needed and weave them, pinning the fabric layers together. Use two pins to hold the two cut edges. Use the placement guide to help determine which path to weave under and over.

Fused and trimmed paths, woven and pinned together, Style A, Fillers One and Five

5. Run a finger above each path to check the overs and unders. The rule of thumb is if a path goes over the first path it encounters, it goes under the next path it encounters (even itself).
6. When completely woven and pinned together, the knot acts as a single unit. Unpin the fabric layers from the placement guide but keep the fabric layers pinned together.
7. Position the knot on its background.
8. Remove the pins and fuse the knot in place.
9. Stitch around the outlines of the knot.

Weave a Celtic Knot Box

(All Styles)

Assemble a Celtic knot and transfer the paths to fabric as shown previously.

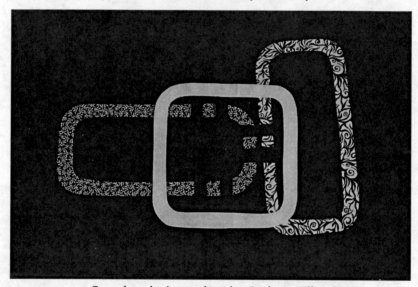

Fused and trimmed paths, Style A, Filler One

The paths of a Celtic knot box can be open loops as shown, or closed loops that have to be cut open before weaving them together. The best place to cut open a path is where it crosses under another path.

Use the assembled templates as a placement guide.

It is best to start at one end of the knot and weave toward the other, row by row.

Look at the bottom row on the placement guide. Notice the path in the lower right corner of the knot lies under the path to the left of it, which lies under the path to the left of it, which lies under the path to the left of it, and so on. This is universal along all four sides of the knot.

1. Position the fused and trimmed path that contains the lower right corner of the knot on the placement guide.
2. Position the fused and trimmed path that lies to the left of the first path on the placement guide. Pin through all layers to anchor them in place.

3. Position each fused and trimmed path on the placement to the left of the previous one until the bottom row is complete.

Fused and trimmed paths laid on placement guide from right to left, Style A, Filler One

4. At the other end of the knot, cut the paths open where they fall "under" another path, then pull the cut ends to where they are anchored.

5. Weave the paths together, row by row, pinning the fabric layers together. Use two pins to hold the two cut edges. Use the placement guide to help determine which path to weave under and over.

6. Run a finger above each path to check the overs and unders. The rule of thumb is if a path goes over the first path it encounters, it goes under the next path it encounters (even itself).
7. When completely woven and pinned together, the knot acts as a single unit. Unpin the fabric layers from the placement guide but keep the fabric layers pinned together.
8. Position the knot on its background.
9. Remove the pins and fuse the knot in place.
10. Stitch around the outlines of the knot.

Templates

Style A Knot End

Style A Knot Corner

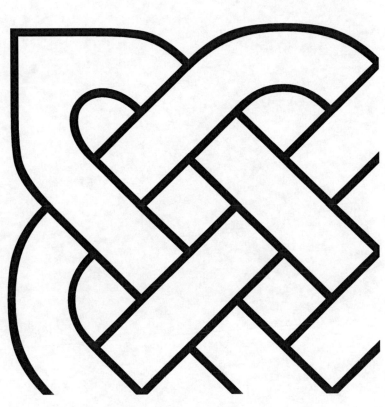

Style B Knot End

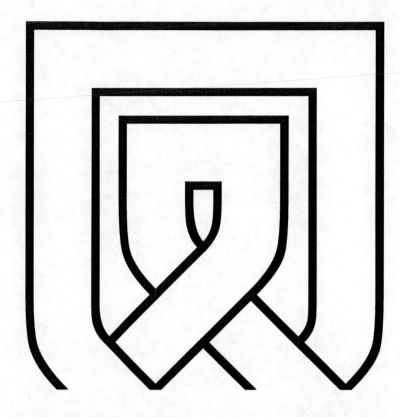

Style B Knot Corner

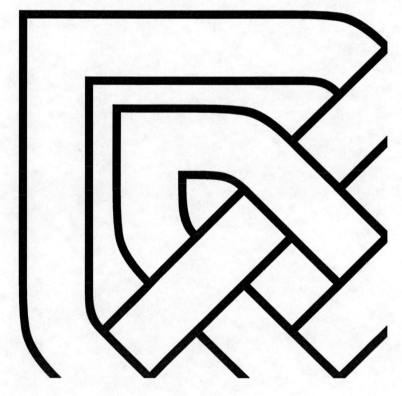

Style C Knot End

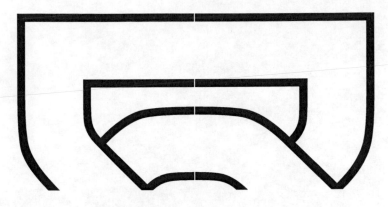

Style C Knot Corner

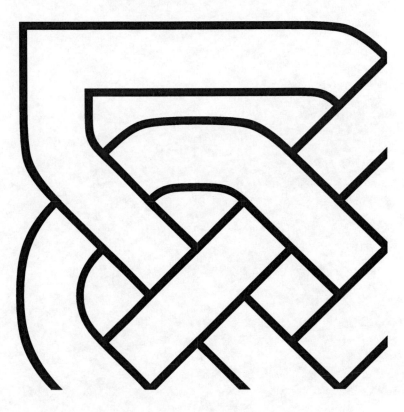

Style D Knot End

Style D Knot Corner

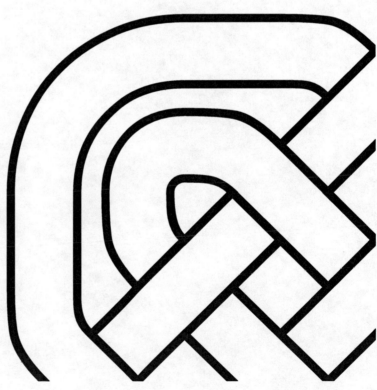

Style E Knot End

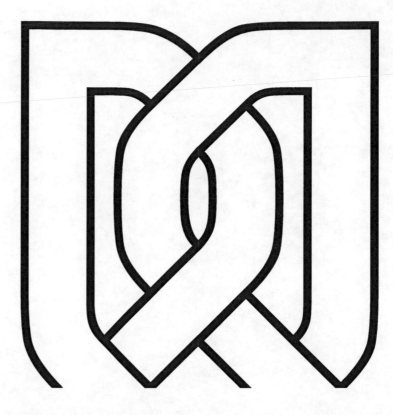

Style E Knot Corner

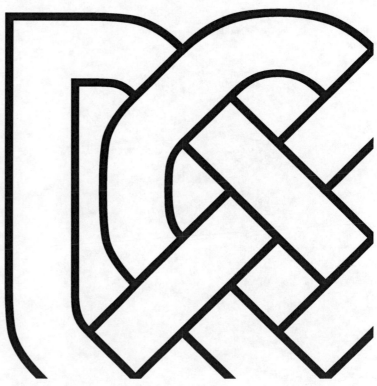

Style F Knot End

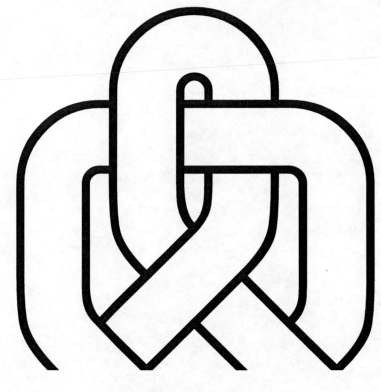

Style F Knot Corner

Filler 1

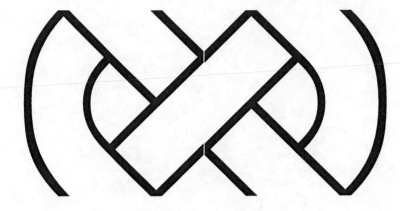

Filler 2

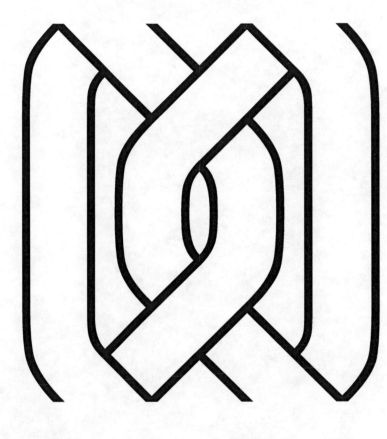

Filler 3

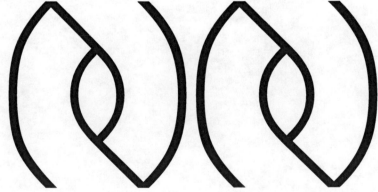

Filler 4

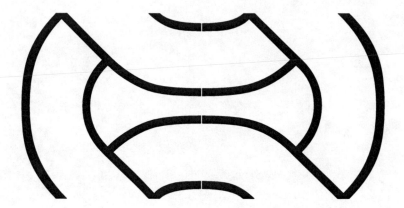

Filler 5

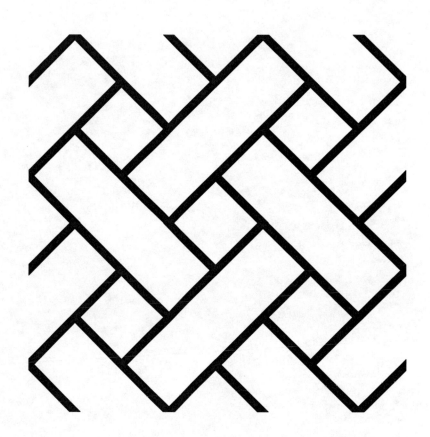

Reversed Templates

Style A Knot End (reversed)

Style A Knot Corner (reversed)

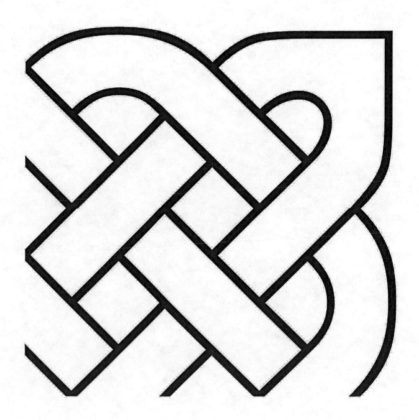

Style B Knot End (reversed)

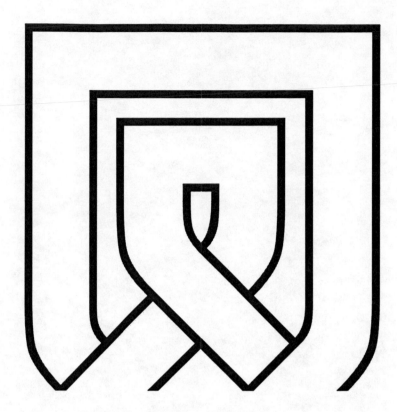

Style B Knot Corner (reversed)

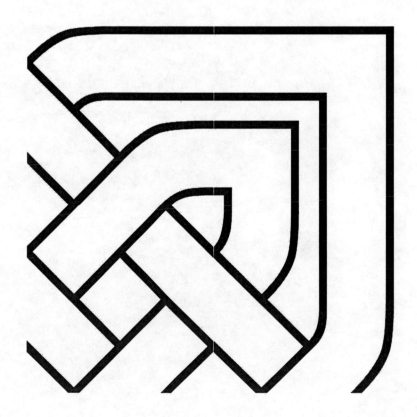

Style C Knot End (reversed)

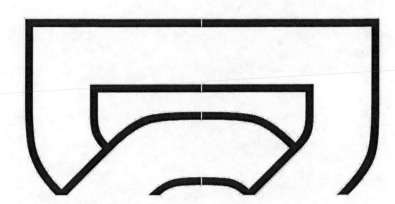

Style C Knot Corner (reversed)

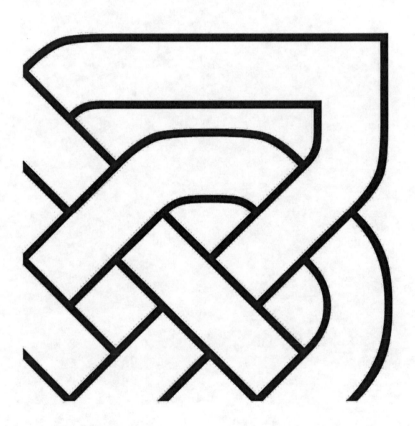

Style D Knot End (reversed)

Style D Knot Corner (reversed)

Style E Knot End (reversed)

Style E Knot Corner (reversed)

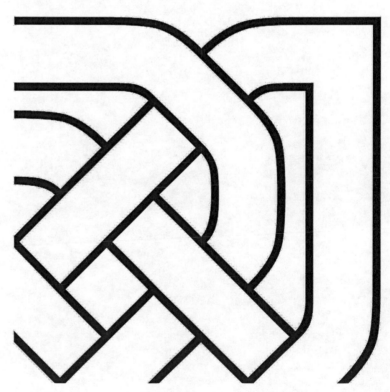

Style F Knot End (reversed)

Style F Knot Corner (reversed)

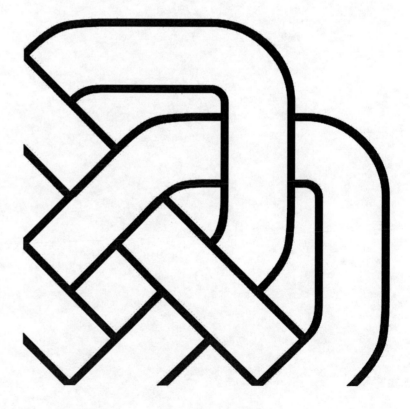

Filler 1 (reversed)

Filler 2 (reversed)

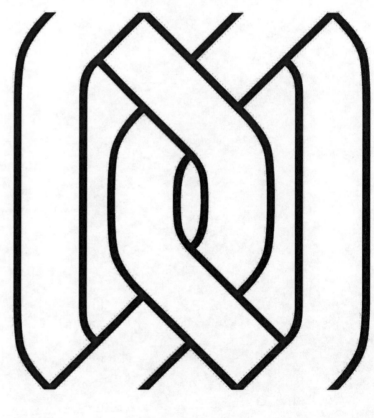

Filler 3 (reversed)

Filler 4 (reversed)

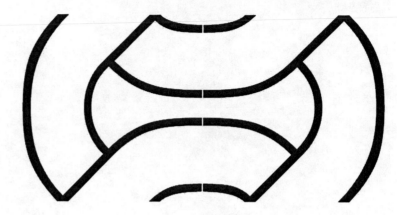

Filler 5 (reversed)

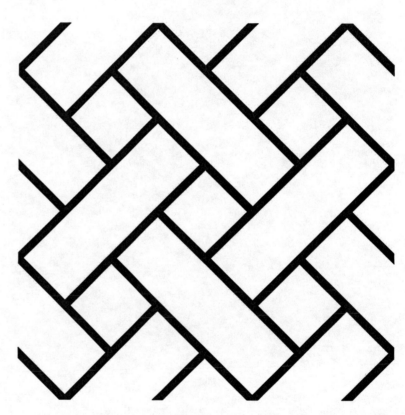

From the Author

I hope you have enjoyed this method of weaving Celtic knots. These are just the basics. Where you take it is up to you.

If you have any comments, questions, or feedback, please contact me at rkh@nachograndmasquilts.com.

Check out my website at www.nachograndmasquilts.com.

Follow me on Facebook www.facebook.com/NachoGrandmasQuilts and Instagram: RaymondKHouston.

Thank you,

Raymond K. Houston

About the Author

Raymond K. Houston is largely self-taught.

He took up sewing on a dare in high school and hand-stitched a black velvet buccaneer shirt as a first project. He sewed clothes for his family until he graduated and moved away, passing the tailoring torch to his father (who Raymond taught to sew).

During America's Bicentennial, Raymond began his first quilt because he felt quilting was Americana. It was machine-pieced, hand-quilted, and took over four years to complete. Once Raymond learned to machine quilt on his domestic sewing machine, he never looked at hand quilting again.

Raymond learned the operations of symmetry and developed a method for generating patchwork patterns of interlocking shapes, called tessellations, which he has demonstrated on TV and taught online. For more than 20 years, he has made quilts using only one patch, yet the quilts never look alike.

His fascination with knotwork is more recent. He is working on original templates for square and hexagonal knotwork.

Raymond has appeared in print and in person around the country, being featured in national quilt magazines and giving talks and workshops to quilt guilds from coast-to-coast. He can be found online on Facebook, Instagram, and his website, NachoGrandmasQuilts.com.

He lives in St. Louis, Missouri. This is his first book.

CPSIA information can be obtained
at www.ICGtesting.com
Printed in the USA
FFOW01n0420070818
47621384-51178FF

9 781939 696380